Crackerjack

Youth Literary & Art Magazine

COURAGE: ISSUE 2

Spring/Summer 2018

Crackerjack Youth & Literary Magazine is published by Kind Eye Publishing, LLC, which is a family owned & operated publishing company that promotes written pieces of work dedicated to the themes of kindness, compassion, diversity and cross cultural communication. Our dream is to spread understanding through our published material, be it through magazines, essays, manuscripts, self-help books, how-to books and more. Our authors represent a diverse ethnic population and voices that may otherwise be unheard.

Find us online!

www.kindeyepublishing.com

facebook.com/kindeyepublishing

"I love trying again and again because I will get better. When I do get better I am so proud of how strong I am."
-Bianca Patel, age 8

"If I see a ghost I can punch them."
-Rowan Lingam, age 4

"I have lots of courage, except when I forget to be brave."
-Naya Patel, age 6

"A shark is brave because it has two eyes and eats fish."
-Nikhil Pradhan, age 3

"Courage is when people do something that they are scared of doing. They just do it!"
-Neil Joshi, age 6

"...I remind myself to be brave, I tell myself, 'I got this.'..."
-Anjali Nagar, age 8

"Having courage is standing up for what is right, even when no one else is."
-Aarya Pradhan, age 6

"Don't be scared, be brave!"
-Sonia Nagar, age 6

"I am brave 561 minutes, then I fizzle like a worm. Then I'm brave again."
-Kishan Patel, age 4

"Courage is going to baseball. I don't always hit the ball, but I go anyway."
-Sohan Desai, age 4

"Brave means to ask for help (to fight a monster)"
-Kai Vadivelu, age 5

"What "courage" means to me is having confidence that what you're doing is right."
-Varun Ashok, age 8

⟨ CONTENTS ⟩

CRACK·ER·JACK

NOUN: CRACKER-JACK

AN EXCEPTIONALLY GOOD PERSON OR THING : a person or thing of special excellence

ACKNOWLEDGMENTS

A special thanks to our contributors. Your words, art and thoughts are important to us and we can't wait to help you get heard. Keep shining bright.

We would also like to acknowledge this issue's sponsors including Crestpoint Companies, Inc., Creative Tots - Mason, Deepali and Mitesh Patel - Realtors, Cincinnati Baila Dance Academy, and Huntington Learning Center. Your support in our youth's creative and academic development is noteworthy and we applaud you. Thank you.

I would also like to thank Sandra Vazquez for her expert design advice and input!

COURAGE

Defining "Courage" has proven to be more thought-provoking and challenging than our previous issue of "Kindness". Our contributors, ranging in ages of 5-16, answered this issue's call with a variety of perspectives. Some focused on how they see courage from within themselves, others on how they have witnessed it in others. The unifying message we see from our crackerjack contributors is this: Courage can be as quiet as a mouse, or as loud as a lion.

I noticed another theme while reviewing the thoughtful submissions for this issue. Our young writers and artists had to really look inward to find the courage to write or draw about such a personal topic. It's hard to admit when you're scared of something, or what you do to overcome that fear. Several writers were asked to dig even deeper, which certainly put them out of their comfort zone. The fact that they all met this challenge only goes to show you how brave and courageous our youth can be.

I couldn't be more proud of them. Read on, you'll see why.

They clearly have something to say.

Let's hear these *crackerjacks* out.

-Avanti Pradhan Vadivelu

Editor's Note

Fear Immobilized

By Andrea Hefferan, 10th grade

I am taking a walk when I hear it

Wailing
Screaming
Moaning

I follow the sound and I see it

Orange
Red
Yellow

My eyes are blinded by the bright colors
They paint the house before they burn it

Heat
Smoke
Flames

Help has yet not arrived to ease it

Where are they?

Can't they hurry?

Hysteria
Panic
Fear

I don't know what I am supposed to do
Why did my walk lead me

Here?

A silhouette
A figure amid the flames
A small hand
Spurs me into action

Hysteria
Panic
Fear

Can't keep me away
I tuck them into
A small corner of my heart
Where they can't bother me

I'm scared senseless
But I know what I need to do

I go in

Coughing
Choking
Crying
I find her easily

Crawling
Quickly
Escape

People call me a hero

They don't know
I almost didn't do it

They ask
How?
But that isn't the right question
They call me
fearless
But that isn't the right word

You never know how
You just know why
You never lose fear
You just learn to ignore it
You learn to have courage

COURAGE
BRAVERY
GO FOR IT
FEARLESS

When I face a fear, I think of it as a challenge and I always conquer a challenge.
-Kavan P. Vadivelu

By Kavan Vadivelu, 5th grade

Dance

By Aashri Parekh, 2nd grade

The first time I started dancing, I felt very scared. I didn't feel like dancing at all. I thought people would make fun of me and I would feel terrible and embarrassed. I also dislike dancing in front of my family, friends, and teachers because I feel nervous and shy. With all those feelings I kept dancing and learning new steps. One day we had to perform on a stage and I felt very nervous but I did it. After our performance, I heard clapping and cheering, nobody was making fun of me. I felt proud and happy. My parents told me that it takes courage to dance in front of so many people and they were very proud.

I Fight

By Rudra Patel, 5th grade

I fight for what I believe. Failing is not on my agenda. Knowing that I might fall I must come back up and fight for what I believe in. Courage infuses me with energy not the energy that you use for everyday tasks, but the energy that everyone has hidden deep within them: the power of belief. Courage is what makes people strive to get back up. There is a myth about courage is that you have to be fearless and confident. But in reality courage means to look straight in to your fear and conquer it. Be brave, be strong, be courageous.

Courage

By Leah Shah, 8th grade

Finishing the race didn't get me here.

Having the courage to start the race and fight through obstacles did.

The greatest power within us is to find our courage.

To move forward and to never give up.

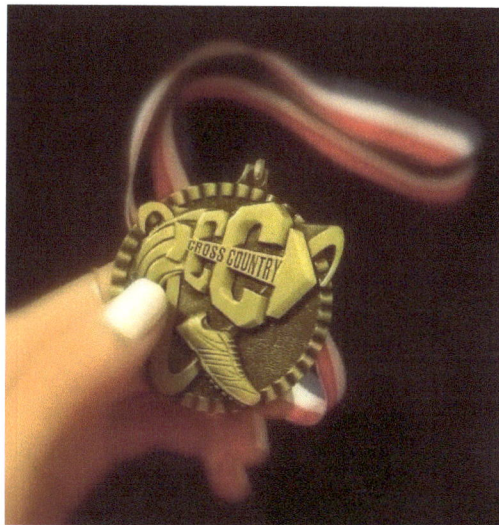

A Week of Courage

By Amrutha Juluri, 4th grade

One Monday, there was a little girl named Violet and she was at school in art class. Violet's teacher said there was going to be an art fair. Her teacher said that each student has to draw a picture and present it. Her teacher also said it was going to be due this Friday. Well, that made Violet nervous. She was very nervous about presenting her drawing because she did not like to talk in front of a lot of people. She needed a way to find more courage.

So, she went home and asked her mom and dad if they could give her any advice.

Her mom said "Draw something that you enjoy so that it is easier to talk about." Her dad said, "Practice makes perfect."

On Tuesday, Violet asked her sister what she could do about the art presentation. Her sister said, "Don't look at the people. Look at the wall and just say your words."

On Wednesday, Violet's friend, Emily, told her, "Act like there is nobody there and speak loud." Violet felt even more nervous and said, "How am I supposed to do that?" Emily showed her by standing up in front of a teacher and speaking loudly.

On Thursday, Violet thought about what everybody said and decided she should give it a try. She practiced just like everyone had taught her. She looked at the wall. She pretended nobody was there, even though there was nobody in her room. And she rehearsed her words, loud.

Friday morning came, and Violet was not nervous. Violet presented her picture and it was OK!!

After that day, Violet was never scared to talk in front of a lot of people again, and that showed courage.

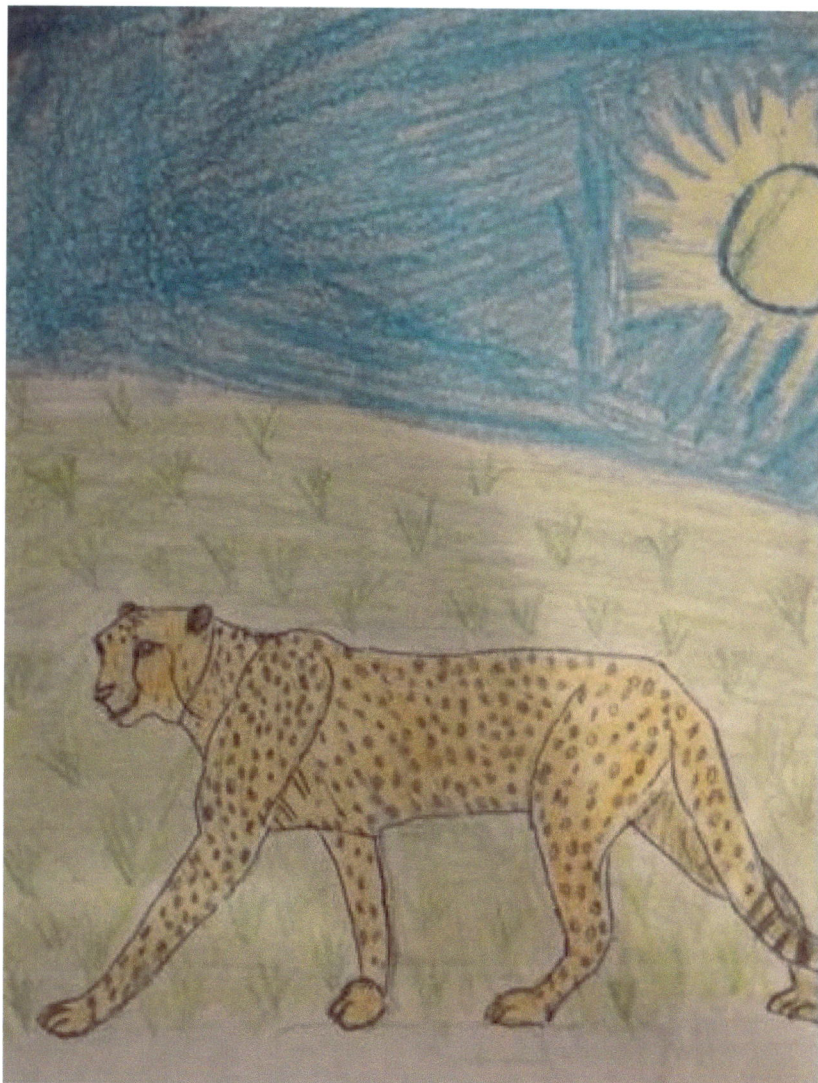

Courage is confidence, like how a cheetah struts.

By Jai Narayan, 7th grade

You Never Know

By Preena Mehta, 4th grade

Courage, to me, is defined as showing bravery towards something that might frighten someone else that also could come back in pain. To have courage is not easy, but you should always stay on your path of courage. Your path of courage is like the journey that supports someone else's heart by the act of courage!

To use courage, you should apologize when you are wrong. Courage can be any little thing that will make you a better person like just as small as being you.

Confronting a bully will really make a difference to the kid getting bullied. Never bully. This could all go wrong! You never know what's going on in their lives.

"Courage allows me to think BIG."
By Rebeca Hefferan, 8th grade

Be Brave

By Anjali Nagar, 2nd grade

I was afraid to go
Scared and frightened
And I've never been there before
I saw people I didn't know
I felt nervous inside
I had nowhere to hide
I whispered, "Be Brave"
I can do this
It took courage to step out onto the court
And it turned out to be fun

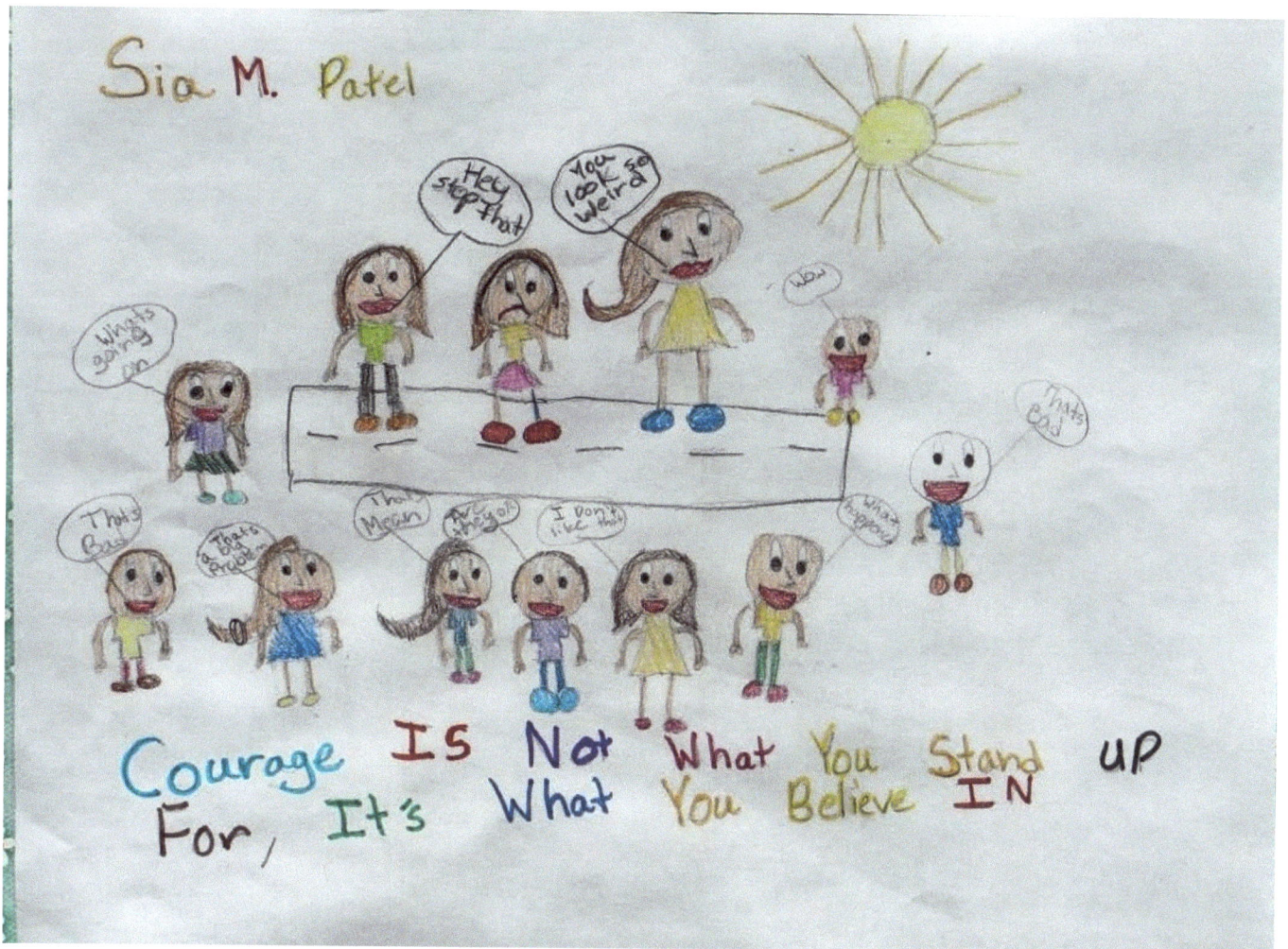

"Courage is Not What You Stand Up For, It's What You Believe In."

By Sia Patel, 4th grade

1,000 and Counting

By Maddie Lin, 10th grade

While brainstorming for this article I had the hardest time trying to figure out what to write about and how to write about it. From frustration I researched the definition of courage to see if I could get any inspiration from it. According to Google, courage is, "The ability to do something that frightens one; strength in the face of pain or grief." Then it hit me. Everyone at a point in their lives needs to have courage. In fact, I'm exhibiting courage right now as I write because I'm afraid that it won't turn out well enough, or that I just can't put my feelings into words.

My whole life I've had stage fright and that has restricted what I could and couldn't do. Whether it was singing karaoke with my friends or performing a small skit in front of my family. At the end of my freshman year, I ran for class officer and now hold the position of sophomore class treasurer. I was up against 15 of my fellow classmates who also wanted to hold the title/position of class officer. For a few years I have been attending this camp called OASC, it has become my second family. It had taught me so many things about being a leader and speaking up. How to be confident when you talk in front of people and this taught me so much that I wasn't afraid when I had to speak in front of a class or other's that I didn't know. All the public speaking had truly been a blessing because I was always too scared to do what I knew I could in front of people and that was talking. I always thought to myself, Come on, you're just talking in front of people why is it so hard? I realized one day that it wasn't the people and the crowd that was freaking me out, it was me that was freaking me out. I was always just psyching myself out and there was no real good reason to why that was. But all of that talking in front of strangers finally led up to the big day.

A couple of months into the year, we had class meetings in our zoo-sized auditorium. The student body president told me and the other class officers a few days before that we had to speak in front of our entire graduating class that afternoon. You can guess what my reaction was upon hearing that. I started to panic and immediately tried to figure out what I would say. I stayed up writing and rewriting with the thought growing in my head that I would mess up and embarrass myself in front of everyone.

When the day came, I had sweaty palms, under-arms and forehead. My friends told me that I would do fine but my fear chose to ignore the supporting comments. When we arrived to the auditorium I turned around to see all the inattentive kids walking in. I sat there trying to calm down, my legs were shaking. I finally heard our introduction, I stood up and smiled. Of course, I thought, I have to be last. My turn came, I took the microphone and spoke. Before I could finish everyone started cheering and the applause filled the auditorium. I could hear my friends scattered around in their seats shouting my name. "Courage, the ability to do something that frightens one." If I have the courage to speak in front of 1,000 people, then I can have the courage to do whatever I believe I can do.

Courage to Ride

By Ryan Shah, 5th grade

Fear of crashing

Fear of injury

Walk away

BREATHE

EXHALE

Push my fears aside

Find the COURAGE to ride

If you see someone geting bullied make sure to stand up for the person geting bullied, that is COURAGE!

By Camila Ariza, 2nd grade

Bianca's Courageous Photo Journal

By Bianca Patel 2nd grade

I am in Destination Imagination. This badge is from my DI team.
I sometimes get scared when I go on stage because I sometimes forget lines, and my voice gets low and I whisper. But this time I talked very loud and that showed courage.

I like to swim. I was little when I started to swim. I was scared and I didn't know how to swim, but I got better and better and better with practice. I kept practicing and never gave up!

This is my Jazz costume. It is from my dance class. I learn jazz, acrobatics and ballet in my class. At home I practice my acrobatics. I need to practice my acrobatics so I can get better. Two girls in my class are really good and they are better at doing the difficult stuff. I can almost do it!

This is my Indian costume. I have to practice my dance every day. Our teacher changes the song every month so it makes it difficult. I do it because I like it a lot. The moves are difficult so I am nervous to perform on stage. I am less nervous because I practice every day.

"I chose to paint a lion to represent courage because they are brave and loyal and both of those things make up courage. You have to stand by your friends and family and defend them when they need help and be happy for them when they are successful. I wanted the lion in this painting to look calm and courageous so I chose the blue colors for the calmness and I painted him staring into the distance to show that he is ready to take on whatever comes his way."

By Gus Hammond, 5th grade

Lemonade Stand

By Keya Vadivelu, 3rd grade

One day Mavey and her friends, Ellie and Addison wanted to run a lemonade stand. They started to build their stand. They called it "Perfect Pink Lemonade". More and more people came. It started to get really hot, but they did not take a break! They wanted to slow down, but there were so many people in the line!

Then, uh oh, Mavey made a little mistake. She spilled the lemonade! Addison got sooo mad! Mavey wished it never happened, but Addison started to yell at poor Mavey. Ellie just tried to stay out of their business.

"That's it." Mavey had enough, "I'm taking a break. Addison you are being a little too rough with your words."

So Mavey took a break. She told her parents what happened and stayed inside for a little bit. Addison and Ellie kept the lemonade stand going without Mavey, but Mavey didn't care because she listened to her heart and found the courage to stay away from friends who make her feel bad. Sometimes, courage means to just listen to your heart.

The End.

Being Brave at School

By Varun Ashok, 2nd grade

What "courage" means to me is having confidence that what you're doing is right. When I was in first grade, I brought my cultural food for lunch. I knew it was the right thing to do. Then at lunch, three people made fun of my lunch. This happened every time I brought cultural food.

I tried to tell them to stop, but it only got worse. I tried telling the teacher and two people stopped commenting, but one person was commenting as strong as the three people who started. I strongly told him to stop, but it was no use. Then I told the teacher again and he stopped. I tried sitting away from them for a couple days. When I sat next to them after that they didn't comment again. Lesson: Never comment on people's food and be courageous to face the situation.

The Midnight Ride

By Mike Devassy, 4th grade

Come, listen to the story of the midnight ride
An event put on history's side.
To stop the British from starting a fight,
Two brave men warned the colonist that night.
Paul Revere and William Dawes
Courageously broke England's laws.
"One if by land, two if by sea,"
The code from lanterns in a church's belfry,
Riding on horses and yelling while running,
"The British are coming! The British are coming!"
Because of Revere and Dawes's quest
Sam Adams and John Hancock evaded arrest.
Dr. Samuel Prescott joins the riders' courses,
And there they were, riding, three men on three horses
The British patrol stops Revere in his tracks
But Dawes and Prescott avoid these setbacks.
These men delivered a message in a night
And Concord and Lexington get ready to fight!
Revere, Dawes, and Prescott too,
Rode that night, under the midnight blue.

Courage at School

By Mahi Patel, 2nd grade

One day at my school kids were putting a heart up on a bulletin board in the hallway for 1,100 reasons why we love our school. Two boys in my class were there and my friend and another girl with her were there also. The two boys started running in the hallways trying to run away from the other girl because she was different from the others and when my friend got back to the classroom she told the teacher everything. Me and my friend heard people whispering about the same girl and me and my friend went over and said STOP TALKING ABOUT OTHER PEOPLE." The boys said, "OK, OK, OK, WE WILL STOP." FROM NOW ON WE STICK UP FOR HER.

The End

Bobby's Triple Dog Dare

By Vishnu Juluri, 2nd grade

There once was a boy whose name was Bobby Cabosky. He asked his dad if he could go to his next-door neighbor Franklin Whizzler's house, to play. Franklin was only three years old and liked to play catch with Bobby. While they were playing they came upon some money in the house. Franklin said, "Let's take this money," but Bobby said, "I don't think so that doesn't sound like a good idea." So Bobby put it in his pocket to take it away from Franklin. He thought it would be better to give it to Mrs. Whizzler later. Bobby felt responsible and brave.

When Bobby got home he took a shower. He forgot he still had the money. He emptied his pockets to show the money to his sister, Lizzie Cabosky.

His dad came in just at that time and said, "What are you doing with all that money!!" Bobby felt scared and worried.

Bobby said nothing. His dad called his mom to come into the room to see what was going on. Bobby really didn't want to get in trouble about *accidentally* taking the money so he decided to tell his parents something else.

He told them he found the money at school. Then they wanted to know **where** he found it, **why** he found it, **who** found it, and **why** he didn't turn it in.

He told them about the mean kid at school. Phoenix Tory had been walking down the hall with Bobby when they spotted some money laying on the floor. Phoenix triple dog dared Bobby to pick up the money and take it home. Bobby said no but Phoenix said that he would embarrass Bobby if he didn't take the money home. So Bobby took the money into his pocket and brought it home.

Bobby's parents took the money and said that he would have to give it back the next morning at school.

The next day Bobby told his mom the actual truth about getting the money away from Franklin.

His mommy asked him, "Why did you lie and make up the story?"

The answer was because he was scared that he was going to get in trouble so he told the lie. Then, he realized if you tell one lie you have to tell another.

Mr. and Mrs. Cabosky decided that Bobby would have to write 100 times - I will not lie to my parents. They also grounded him for two weeks.

Bobby was sure that he would never tell a lie ever again in is whole life. Courage means to tell the truth, even if you are scared.

Kindness is Happiness

By Vishnu Juluri, 2nd grade

You have to show courage when you play basketball. You should never be scared to lose.

You have to show courage by talking in front of hundreds of people.

You have to show courage when you get married, because you will be joining another family.

You have to show courage by letting people try your best food.

You have to show courage by writing a big story and not messing up.

You have to show courage by taking a class for the first time.

You have to show courage when getting your ears pierced.

You have to show courage when someone delivers a baby.

You have to show courage by building a big house.

You have to show courage by starting a new job.

You have to show courage by talking on TV as a newscaster.

Courage for Cardinal

By Elisa Hefferan, 3rd grade

I looked grumpily out the car window and wished I could just be invisible. Today, wasn't just bad, it was horrible! Three days ago, I moved to this little town, Altadois. Now, I was going to AMS for fifth grade. As I walked into the school, I had a feeling of dread.

I peeked around the corner of the new homeroom and looked around. There were kids laughing and playing around like old buddies. "Sure does look I have a lot of catching up to do," I thought glumly as I slid into my seat.

"Hello class!" I looked up from my seat. It was my new teacher! She sounded like a very shrill owl. "Attendance!" Oh no! Not attendance! I'm always first, and I hate it! I hope I'm not first. "Anabeca?" I raised my hand. I heard snickers behind me. "Anabeca?" "Here" I mumbled "Oh, okay just say something next time." "Okay." I didn't hear anyone else's name, because I put my head down for the rest of homeroom.

"It's hard to be lonely in such a big school, don't you think?" I looked up, startled. I was on my way to math and no one had talked to me since homeroom. It was a girl from my homeroom. She had a blue hair, (probably dyed), which was in a funky side ponytail, and deep, dark, blue eyes. "Um...yeah...

well…ah…hi…" I stammered, sure she would laugh at me. But she didn't. She just smiled at me and said "Hi. My name is Randrea, what's yours?" "Ana..Anabeca" I replied softly. "Nice name!" She said. "Yeah… thanks… where are your other friends?" I asked. "Oh, my friend moved, to a school called Brookhood, I think." she paused, "She was a good friend, Cecilia was her name." Randrea told me. "Well, what good is it just standing here? Let's go! What's your next class?" "Math," I answered "Cool! Same here!" And for the first time in the day, I laughed merrily as Randrea pulled me in the halls.

"I can't believe I survived my first day of school," I thought. Randrea was in the same neighborhood as me, so we were on the same bus. The school day seemed to pass really quickly, and Randrea and I were talking. "You know, your hair and your dress kind of remind of a bright red cardinal." Randrea observed. I blushed and looked up at my red wavy hair, then at my bright red dress. "I have a great idea! Since you remind of a cardinal, your nickname should be Cardinal!" Randrea told me excitedly. "Yeah! And your nickname should be…" I stopped "what could Randrea's nickname be?" I thought. I looked up at Randrea's funky, blue, ponytail. "Your nickname should be Blue Jay!" I nearly shouted. "Okay, Cardinal. Blue Jay sounds cool." Randrea, I mean Blue Jay, said, winking. "Nice choice, Blue Jay" I replied, winking back. We both burst out of laughter. We were both giggling delightfully when Randrea stopped giggling. "Can you be my new best friend?" She suddenly asked. "What?" I asked, and I too stopped giggling. "I would love to, but isn't Cecilia already your best friend?" I asked. Blue Jay smiled "Well, yeah, but I can have more than one best friend, right?" She said eagerly. I nodded. "Well, what do you say?" she asked. I smiled "YES!" I said loudly. And I jumped up and hugged Blue Jay. We started laughing again. Suddenly, with Blue Jay at my side, I felt I had more courage.

Veteran

By Kavan Vadivelu, 5th grade

Brave, bold, mighty, and strong
Always fights against the wrong

When all is lost they bring back the light
Because they know what is right
And they will always make things bright

Though you might not know that they are there
They will always fill you with care
Though they are as brave as a bear
Their kindness is never rare

Our Volunteer Vacation

By Dharma Patel, 9th grade

Growing up as a third generation Indian American, our parents have always made the effort to help us stay in touch with our Indian roots while still living the western lifestyle. One of the many important values our parents have taught us is the notion of volunteerism and giving back. Together we have made many volunteer trips, such as to a Native American reservation in Seattle and to Mexico.

Our most recent trip was to India in December 2017. One of the scariest things about going to a third world country like India is not being able to know what to expect. We had to learn how to be prepared with some of the unknowns that could happen and become aware that anything could happen. Therefore, before we went to India we had to get a series of shots to protect us from the potential illnesses that could happen. As we were listening to the different things that could happen, it scared us but we made a decision that we still wanted to go on our trip. This is when we realized that our parents had been challenging us with different things in life so that we would have the confidence and courage to be able to commit to this kind of a trip.

We started our journey to India on December 22nd by arriving in New Delhi. The first few days of our trip were spent learning about the history of this beautiful country. We learned about different monuments such as the Red Fort(s), the Taj Mahal, and the history behind New Delhi. Then, we flew to Bardoli which is in the state of Gujarat and started the volunteer part of our trip.

The first school we visited was an all-boys Ashram, SumitraBa School Anaval, and Gujarat. We sat down in a large room with all the kids and did yoga, pranayam, mediations, and listened to speeches about overcoming obstacles in life. The kids performed Gujarat's culture dance called Dangi Dance and we performed a jump rope routine and had the boy's and even some of the teachers come and jump in the ropes. My sister and I are on the Comet Skippers Jump Rope Team and have been performing and competing for over five years and it is a great way to bring people together from different countries and cultures together. Afterwards, we had the privilege of serving food to all the young boys. We noticed that as the boys grabbed food and sat down, not one of them started to eat until every one of them sat down. Then, they said a prayer/grace which translated to "we all eat together, we all pray together, we all sleep together, and that will keep us together." Only after this did they start to eat. We were in awe of these kids because they had so much discipline and respect for one another.

After lunch, we went outside the playground area, to plant about fifty trees so that the kids could stay cool in India's scorching heat. After planting trees, we made our way to a playing field much like a football field and the young boys taught us a game that they like to play during their free time. The game was called "Kho Kho". We all had so much fun playing together, and laughing as my sister and I completely kept losing. We later had the chance to give every single one of the kids a backpack to use for school. It warmed our hearts to see their faces light up as we handed out the backpacks along with american chocolates. To the kids, us being there and giving them backpacks was a gift. But the real gift was to us given the opportunity to serve these kids. Being able to give back and play with these kids was such a reward to us and we will never forget how grateful the kids were when we handed them the backpacks.

The next day, we visited an all-girls school and met a lady, who everyone referred to as Mataji. When translated, Mataji means "mother" or "grandmother". She told us her story and how this school (Sardar Vidhyalaya Ashram) came to be. Mataji goes around to different small and poor villages in the surrounding regions and handpicks girls who are not wealthy and don't have an education. She takes them back to the school to provide the education that is needed for them. It was inspiring to see her empower the girls so they can be more than housewives, while earning an education and learning the life skills so they could go back to their villages and teach those skills to others. Some of things they were learning were to make furniture, sewing and cooking.

With the language barrier, we couldn't converse, so instead, my sister and I decided to grab our jump ropes and have the girls jump. It was incredible how even though we couldn't talk to each other, we could still understand each other through jump rope. They would get in, jump a bit, laugh a little and then I'd give them a high five telling them they did a great job. They were having so much fun that when we had to stop jumping all the girls' faces dropped a bit. We left some ropes in the hopes that they can still jump rope even after we left. Since the girls could not go out to eat at restaurants we decided to bring the restaurant to them. We catered in some pav bhaji and served them. After we served all the girls we sat down with some of them and although we didn't know how to speak perfect Gujarati we made small conversations. Being able to eat on the floor with the girls and ask them what they want to be when they grow up or what they like to do in their free time had to have been our favorite part of visiting this school.

The blind and physically disabled Ashram was our next stop. We entered the school and sat down to watch a small program that the kids put on for us. The best part of this program was seeing how these kids treated each other. The partially blind kids would grab the hand of completely blind kids and help them up to the stage. Seeing these kids act with such kindness towards one another made our hearts warm. The kids aren't embarrassed to get help or to help others but instead they were confident in who they were as individuals. After the program and serving them dinner; my sister, our friends and I saw that there was a group of girls that were talking. We decided to go talk to them, and asked each other some questions so that we could get to know them better. They wanted to listen to some American music, so we grabbed a speaker and took it up to them. They led us to a room where we played the music and all of a sudden they grabbed our hands and started to dance. In no time, there was music playing with a room full of girls dancing and laughing with so much joy and happiness.

This trip changed our perspective on life and made us appreciate our roots so much more than we had in the past. The kids at these schools don't have a fancy mattress to sleep on, they don't have iPhones to play on when they are bored, and they don't have a couch to lounge on while watching TV. But what they did have, was much more than any of us care to recognize in our own lives. They have happiness, they have discipline, they have respect, and these kids are grateful for the small things in life that we take for granted. Every school that we visited showed us that we have been taking many things for granted. They don't get to go home to their parents and say I love you and give them a hug. But we have this, and yet we come home and just walk right past our parents with our heads down stuck in our phones. This trip has taught us to be a human. TO BE a human is different than BEING a human. Being human is having the form of a human. But, to be a human is to open your hearts to others by feeding the hungry, serving the elders, educating the poor, and helping the less fortunate. That takes courage.

By Natalia Ariza, 7th grade

The Small Fish: A Sea Story

By Aarya Pradhan, 1st grade

Once there was a small fish who lives at the bottom of the sea. She never showed herself to humans. One day, though, she didn't know but she had to put on a show for the humans. She was surprised, but then she knew she could do it because she had courage and believed in herself. She went and performed her act to the humans and they loved it. They were even yelling to perform again, "ONE MORE TIME, ONE MORE TIME!"

The End

What is Courage?

By Roshan Mehta, 7th grade

What is courage?

Courage is standing up, not standing down

To help someone if they are getting bullied

Courage is helping a companion

No matter who the bully is in relation to

you

Courage is being there for someone

Through their ups and downs

Courage is being brave and fearless

Courage is something

You give and take

Courage

By Dev Patel, 1st grade

Courage to me means being brave. I was trying out for the Water Moccasins Swim team. The pool was 12 feet deep. My mom wanted me to swim in it but I didn't. I was scared in the beginning but then I decided to be brave and I jumped in. I was happy that I tried and made it on the team.

CRACKERJACK CONTRIBUTORS

Camila Ariza, Artist

Camila is a sweet 8 yearold girl that loves gymnastics, drawing, reading and being with friends. She loves spaghetti and pink lemonade. When she grows up she would like to be an actress.

Natalia Ariza, Artist

Natalia is 12 years old and goes to Mason City Schools. She enjoys drawing in her free time and is involved with cross country, guard and dance. She hopes to one day work as a concept artist for Pixar.

Varun Ashok, Columnist

Varun is in second grade and attends Mason City Schools. He loves his school and says it is full of fun and challenges. He loves art, conducting science experiments, math and music. In his spare time between tennis, piano, Carnatic vocal and swimming lessons, he loves playing with his Nintendo switch!

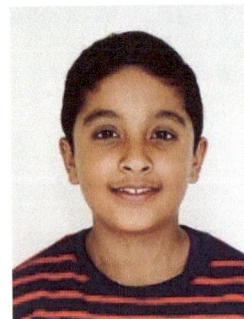

Mike DeVassy, Poet

Mike is a fourth grader at Mason City Schools and was born in Massachusetts, which makes the story of Revere very special to him. Reading and music are his passions, and he recently posted his 40th book review on his school blog! Mike was the Spelling Bee school champion in 3rd grade and apart from reading, he plays guitar, sings in the church choir, and takes part in musical theater, performing as Sher Khan in "Jungle Book", and in 'Mary Poppins'.

Andrea Hefferan, Poet

Andrea Hefferan is a sophomore at Mason High School. She enjoys reading and writing very much. She writes for her high school's newspaper, The Chronicle. Playing music is one of her favorite activities; she plays the violin and piano. In her free time, you can find her reading a book or listening to songs from the musical Hamilton.

Elisa Hefferan, Short Story Writer

Elisa Hefferan is a third grader at Mason City Schools and loves writing, reading, and drawing. She also enjoys roller skating, dancing, and playing the piano. She has two sisters and an amazing mom and dad. Her pet is a turtle named Sheldon whose magic trick is climbing out of his tank. She has some wonderful friends who always support her. This is her first publication. She is so glad to be writing for Crakerjack.

Rebeca Hefferan, Artist

Rebeca Hefferan is an eighth grader at Mason City Schools and is a middle child with an older and younger sister. Rebeca plays the bass and the piano. She enjoys reading, writing and drawing in her free time. Rebeca loves history and science, and loves listening to music. She's always doodling on something, and never far away from a creative idea.

Gus Hammond, Artist

Gus Hammond is 11 years old and lives in Cincinnati, OH. He currently plays water polo and is a member of a local Boy Scout troop as well as being a part of Destination Imagination. In his free time, he likes to ride bikes, cook, and watch YouTube.

Amrutha Juluri, Short Story Writer

Amrutha is 9 years old. Her favorite classes are art and music. Blue and green are her two favorite colors. Most of all, she likes to sing and dance.

Vishnu Juluri, Poet/Short Story Writer

Vishnu is in second grade and is 8 years old. He likes basketball and swimming. My favorite things to do are drawing and fixing things with his Dad.

Maddie Lin, Columnist

Maddie Lin is a 15 year old sophomore at William Mason High School. She's always enjoyed writing and found it was a great outlet for her. Maddie is her graduating lasses' treasurer, she has been playing piano for 10 years, she's on a competitive dance team and she loves to sing. She's so thankful for this opportunity and thanks Avanti and wishes Crackerjack the best of luck!

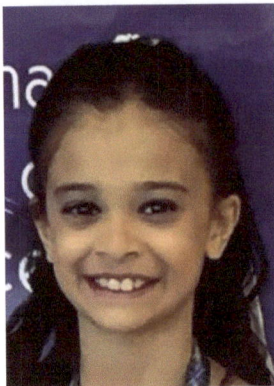

Preena Mehta, Columnist

Preena is a fourth grader at Mason City Schools who enjoys playing sports, doing crafts, and hanging out with her friends. She lives at home with her mom, dad, brother and "little sister" puppy.

Roshan Mehta, Poet

Roshan is a seventh grader who enjoys playing sports, hanging out with his friends, and drawing. He lives with his mom, dad, little sister, and his "littlest sister" puppy.

Anjali Nagar, Poet

Anjali Nagar is 8 years old and is a second grader at Mason City Schools. She has one younger sister, three fish and a new puppy named Taj. In her spare time she enjoys doing crafts, comedy, reading fiction books, swimming, Bollywood dance and ballet, playing volleyball. Most of all she enjoys spending time with her family and friends.

Jai Narayan, Artist

Jai is 12 years old and loves to hang out with his friends. He also enjoys spending time with his dog and family. He likes to be outside and likes to play soccer with his team.

Bianca Patel, Photojournalist

Bianca was born in Louisville Kentucky on April 24, 2010 and moved when she was a baby to Mason, Ohio. Her family members include her mom, dad, little sister and little brother. Almost her entire family lives in Georgia, of which she is the oldest cousin. Bianca loves to read, dance, play tennis and play with her friends.

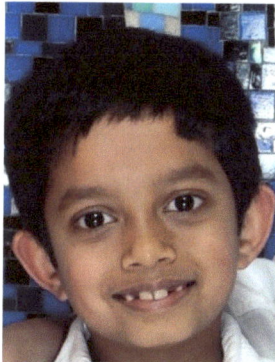

Dev Patel, Columnist

Dev Patel is a first grader who is beginning to really enjoy reading! He loves reading and writing non-fiction stories, mainly based on animals. He is currently reading the Magic Tree House series. In his spare time Dev is a Cub Scout, swimmer, Bollywood dancer and little brother.

Dharma Patel, Columnist

Dharma is 14 years old in the ninth grade at William Mason High School in Ohio. She is a competitive jump roper for the Comet Skippers and is involved in a couple of clubs at her school. She loves to travel and has been on many mission/volunteer trips, which she enjoys so much!

Mahi Patel, Short Story Writer

Mahi is 8 years old and is in second grade. Her favorite color is blue. She loves to play outside and enjoys playing board games and to work on Google drawings.

Rudra Patel, Columnist

Rudra loves to read and write newspaper articles and finds many very interesting. He is a Boy Scout, swims competitively and enjoys playing video games and researching newly introduced technology, using some of this knowledge on his competitive Lego Robotics team. This is his second time contributing to Crackerjack and is very excited to share his writing piece.

Sia Patel, Artist

Sia is nine years old and is in fourth grade. She loves to read fiction books, draw and color. In her free time she likes writing short stories. Her favorite color is pink.

Aashri Parekh, Columnist

Aashri loves to dance, swim, read and draw. She has a younger brother whom she loves to play with. This is her first time contributing to Crackerjack!

Aarya Pradhan, Short Story Writer

Aarya is six years old (going on 16) and is in first grade. Aarya stays busy with dance, piano, Kids' Theater and her crafts, such as making potions. Her latest hobby is writing short stories and play scripts. When she's not busy with all her hobbies she loves spending time with her two little brothers.

Leah Shah, Poet

Leah Shah is 13 years old and in eighth grade at Mason City Schools. In her spare time she loves to write short stories, read, and loves to create apps for her cell phone. Leah runs cross country. She is looking forward to going to high school and to see what other possibilities are out there for her to explore.

Ryan Shah, Poet

Ryan is an 11 year old fifth grader and attends Mason City Schools. Ryan's passion is cartoon illustration and car racing. He recently joined a go kart racing league, and absolutely enjoys it. Ryan is young "Rembrandlt" and is exploring his artistic abilities.

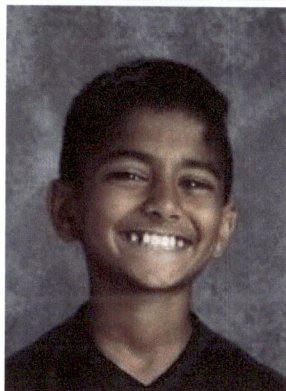

Kavan Vadivelu, Poet/Artist

Kavan is a fifth grader and loves soccer, drawing, acting and singing. Some of his favorite roles include the Jungle Book's Mowgli, Aladdin and Charlie Bucket in "Willy Wonka and the Chocolate Factory". Kavan loves being part of his Destination Imagination team where he can put his creativity, leadership and teamwork skills to the test.

Keya Vadivelu, Short Story Writer

Keya is a third grader who one day hopes to be a fashion designing animal rights activist who lives on a farm. Her passion to "save the earth" can be witnessed on her YouTube Channel, "Kiki's Trash Talk". She has a voracious reading appetite, enjoys jump rope and dance, and loves to play with her two brothers, cousins, friends and dog named Lola.

Call for Submissions!

"Compassion."

What is 'Compassion'?

We are looking for all types of entries from young crackerjacks.

- Art
- Poetry
- Short Story
- Photography
- Essay

Get your voices heard.

Submission Fee is $10 and includes writing advice from professional writer/editor, copy of publication, online recognition, sales/distribution of print magazine, group sessions and launch event.
Discounts for multiple entries may apply.

Send check payable to: "Kind Eye Publishing" KIND EYE PUBLISHING, LLC Attn: SUBMISSION PO Box 511 Mason, OH 45040	Send submissions electronically (artwork must be in jpeg format) to: avanti@kindeyepublishing.com Artwork may also be sent to: PO Box 511 Mason, OH 45040

Submission Deadline August 1, 2018

www.ingramcontent.com/pod-product-compliance
Lightning Source LLC
Chambersburg PA
CBHW040020050426
42452CB00002B/63